The Holy Prophet's ﷺ Kingdom

How much did Allah ﷻ grant His Most Beloved ﷺ?

by

Mufti Ahmed Yaar Khan Na'īmi Ashrafi ؒ

THE HOLY PROPHET'S ﷺ KINGDOM

All Rights Reserved. No part of this book may be reproduced or transmitted by any means, electronic or mechanical, without written permission from the publisher.

Translation of *Sultanat'e-Mustapha* ﷺ *dar Mumlikat'e-Kibriyaa* by Mufti Ahmed Yaar Khan Na'īmi Ashrafi ؏ – 2nd Edition (2013)

Published by	Islamic Lifestyle Solutions Durban, South Africa www.islamiclifestylesolutions.co.za
Translated by	Mufti Omar Dawood Qadri Moeeni Durban, South Africa

We would also like to thank Junaid Yaseen for all of his assistance and support rendered towards the completion of this work.

ISBN 978-0-620-56050-4

Find more books at www.islamic-literature.com

CONTENTS

Author's Note   5

Introduction   17

Chapter 1 – Proof of the Holy Prophet's ﷺ Kingdom

    From the Holy Quran   19

    From the Hadith   24

    Verdicts of the Islamic Scholars   35

    Rational Proofs   41

Chapter 2 – Objections & Answers   45

بسم الله الرحمن الرحيم

الصلوة و السلام عليك يا رسول الله ﷺ

Author's Note

The kings of this world set the rules, procedure and protocol of entering and being in their courts, and they enforce these rules on the general public through their appointed governors and ministers. "When you enter my court, stand like this, speak in this manner, greet like so, etc." they decree. The king rewards those who observe the protocol and punishes those who act contrary to it. However, these rules on how to behave in the presence of a king are applicable to humans alone. Jinns, angels, animals, etc. are not obliged to follow them because a king doesn't have authority over them. When he dies, his court (as well as his rules) end and a new set then emerges.

Nevertheless, there is a court on this earth whose etiquette has been ordained by Allah ﷻ Himself. How to enter it, speak in it, greet by presenting Salaam, etc. have all been decreed by Him. Allah ﷻ commands His servants, "When you enter this court, be mindful of its refinement and ceremony. If you prove to be unbecoming in it, you will be severely punished." The gracefulness of this court is such that even though our eyes cannot visibly see its pomp and glory and its king has taken leave from us, its etiquette still remains and has to be observed. In fact, it's not only obligatory on us alone – this court's dominion is so expansive that even angels are not allowed to enter it without permission; jinns humbly present themselves therein; animals prostrate to it; lifeless trees and stones recite its Kalima; the sun & moon enter rapture if they receive even a gesture from its master, and clouds send showers of mercy at its master's behest. In short, every worldly and Heavenly being is a humble servant of this powerful dominion. Muslims! Do you know who this court belongs to? It is none other than the powerful and authoritative beloved of Allah ﷻ, the intercessor of sinners, the Mercy unto Creation, Sayyiduna Ahmad-e-Mujtaba, Muhammad Mustapha ﷺ.

Friends, let us first see how the Holy Quran teaches us the etiquette of this court:

1. During the time of the Holy Prophet ﷺ, some would make *qurbaani* before him and some would begin fasting before the commencement of Ramadaan. In reply, Allah ﷻ said,

یا ایھا الذین آمنوا لا تقدموا بین یدی اللہ و رسولہ و اتقوا اللہ ان اللہ سمیع علیم

"O Believers. Do not commit any excess before Allah ﷻ & His Messenger ﷺ; and fear Allah ﷻ. Surely Allah ﷻ hears, knows."
– Surah Hujaraat, Verse 1

This verse teaches us respect; that a Muslim must not precede the Holy Prophet ﷺ in speech, walking or anything else.

2. In another example, there was a companion of the Beloved Prophet ﷺ by the name of Hadrat Thaabit ibn Qais ibn Shamaas ؓ who was hard of hearing. Whenever he came to the court of Allah's Messenger ﷺ, he would speak in a raised voice. How could Allah ﷻ allow anyone to speak to His Beloved ﷺ in such a way?! So, He said,

یا ایھا الذین آمنوا لا ترفعوا اصواتکم فوق صوت النبی و لا تجھروا لہ بالقول
کجھر بعضکم لبعض ان تحبط اعمالکم و انتم لا تشعرون

"O Believers. Do not raise your voices above the voice of the Prophet ﷺ and don't speak aloud in his presence the way you speak aloud amongst one another lest your deeds be in vain while you are unaware."
– Surah Hujaraat, Verse 2

Subhanallah! Those who present themselves in this court aren't even allowed to raise their voices!

After this verse was revealed, Hadrat Thaabit ؓ stopped attending the blessed gatherings out of fear. One day, Rasoolullah ﷺ said, "Thaabit ؓ hasn't come for a few days." The Companions then went to his house and enquired as to the reason for his absence. He explained, "I've become Jahannami (an inmate of Hell) because of my loud voice. The verse attests to this." When this was relayed back to the Holy Prophet ﷺ, he replied, "He is a Jannati (an inmate of Jannah)." (In other words, whatever was previously done was forgiven).

Following this verse, Hadrat Abu Bakr, Umar and some other Companions ؓ adopted such a soft tone in their conversations with the Prophet ﷺ that he had to ask them to repeat themselves several times. The following was also revealed about them,

ان الذين يغضون اصواتكم عند رسول الله اولئك الذين امتحن الله قلوبهم للتقوى لهم مغفرة و اجر عظيم

"Undoubtedly those who lower their voices in the presence of the Messenger of Allah ﷺ are the ones whose hearts Allah ﷻ has tested for piety. For them is forgiveness and a great reward."
– Surah Hujaraat, Verse 3

3. Some people from the Tameem tribe once came to the Holy Prophet's ﷺ court at noon while he was resting. They began to shout from outside, which was an act unbearable to Allah ﷻ. When even Hadrat Jibrael عليه السلام doesn't enter without permission, how can people shout while outside?! The following was immediately revealed,

ان الذين ينادونك من وراء الحجرات اكثرهم لا يعقلون

"Certainly many of those who call you from behind your private apartments have no understanding."
– Surah Hujaraat, Verse 4

Allah ﷻ then teaches etiquette and respect in the very next verse,

"And if they had patience until you (O Beloved ﷺ) had come out to them, that would have been better for them. And Allah ﷻ is Forgiving, Merciful."
– Surah Hujaraat, Verse 5

The form of respect taught here is that if a person comes to the Prophet ﷺ while he's in his blessed home, he mustn't shout and call him out. Rather, he must patiently wait for him. Only when the blessed master emerges from his chamber may one greet and speak to him.

4. Rasoolullah ﷺ made nikah to Ummul-Mu'mineen Sayyidah Zainab ؓ and extended a general invitation for the *waleemah* (wedding feast). His Companions came, ate in groups and then left. Three people, however, remained seated after completing their meal. By not realizing how long they were taking, their conversation was starting to become lengthy. Since the blessed house was small, the Prophet ﷺ became inconvenienced by their sitting but still refrained

from asking them to leave (due to his merciful nature). Nevertheless, Allah ﷻ revealed,

> "O Believers. Do not enter the houses of the Prophet ﷺ unless you attain permission for a meal, not waiting for its preparation. Yes. When you are invited, then enter, and when you have taken your meal, disperse; not that you may sit and amuse yourselves in talk."
> – Surah Ahzaab, Verse 53

We can ascertain from this verse that the etiquette of partaking in an invitation in the prophetic court is that one should not present himself there before the meal is prepared or remain seated after eating. Why is this so? The Holy Quran explains,

> "Surely this was causing inconvenience to the Prophet ﷺ and he had regard for you. But Allah ﷻ is not shy of speaking the truth."
> – Surah Ahzaab, Verse 53

5. It was the practice of the Sahaabah to say, "Raa'inaa, O Prophet of Allah ﷺ!" if they couldn't understand any of his utterances. The saying means, "O Prophet ﷺ, repeat what you just said so that we may understand it." However, the word 'Raa'inaa' was also an expression of insolence in the language of the Jews. So, intending *their* meaning of the word, the Jews began to use it and were content in insulting the Noble Messenger ﷺ in this way. How could Allah ﷻ however, the Knower of All Things, allow His Beloved ﷺ to be ridiculed in this manner? He says,

> "O You who believe. Don't say 'Raa'inaa' (to My Messenger ﷺ), but say 'Unzurnaa' and listen attentively from the onset. And a painful punishment is for the disbelievers."
> – Surah Baqarah, Verse 104

Rasoolullah's ﷺ court is such a respected one that even uttering a word which can be misused is not allowed in it.

6. At a certain time, it unexpectedly occurred that the conversations of wealthy Muslims with the Prophet ﷺ became so lengthy that poor Muslims could not get a chance to speak to him. So, the following verse was revealed,

> "O Believers, when you consult the Messenger ﷺ, offer something in charity before your consultation."
> – Surah Mujaadalah, Verse 12

Subhanallah! If you wish to converse with Allah ﷻ (i.e. perform Salaah), making wudhu is sufficient, but if you wish to speak with the Beloved of Allah ﷺ, charity must be given first. There are two benefits to this,

a. By this rule being emplaced, destitute Muslims could also attain a chance to speak in the Holy Prophet's ﷺ court.

b. The respect of this court would be set in the heart because whatever is attained after spending and strife is cherished and honoured.

Even though this verse was annulled later on, the glory of the Holy Prophet ﷺ is still recognized through it.

7. Allah ﷻ didn't keep His Beloved ﷺ in Makkah Sharif but in Madina Munawwara, a place approximately 300 miles away, since He did not wish for anyone to visit the sacred Rauda (resting place) through the means of Hajj. Rather, a separate journey would have to be undertaken for it. So, the importance of visiting this blessed court is established here. Allah ﷻ states,

> "O Believers, respond to the call of Allah ﷻ and the Messenger when the Messenger ﷺ calls you."
> – Surah Anfaal, Verse 24

This verse teaches us that we are to immediately respond to the calling of the Prophet ﷺ as soon as his blessed voice is heard by us, no matter what we are doing. Naturally, the Sahaabah acted upon this command too, and those who wish to read more on this topic may refer to my book, *Shaan'e-Habibur-Rahman*. It includes an incident wherein a Companion, while reading Salaah, broke it to present himself in front of the Prophet ﷺ on hearing his call. There are several other incidents like this. Alahazrat Imam Ahmed Raza Khan ؓ states,

> 'It's proven that all other obligations are secondary. The primary principle of servitude is reserved for that king (Rasoolullah ﷺ).'

These few verses in which the respect of the Holy Prophet ﷺ is taught were only presented as examples. If these and other verses are comprehensively explained, journals would be required. Incidentally, the reward Allah ﷻ bestows to those fortunate people who demonstrate respect and reverence has also been mentioned in the previous verses. We know that those who are respectful to the Prophet ﷺ have been promised forgiveness, are bestowed piety, that Allah ﷻ is pleased with them and that they are with Him. In short, the Holy Quran mentions their praise in several places. I do not wish to go into detail about Allah's ﷻ anger incurred by those who are insolent and disrespectful to the Holy Prophet ﷺ. Only two incidents regarding this are presented below:

1. The non-Muslim Waleed ibn Mugheera once called the Holy Prophet ﷺ a lunatic, bringing sorrow into the heart of the Messenger ﷺ and stirring Divine anger. As a result, Surah Qalam was revealed to the Prophet ﷺ for his consolation, and his excellences were mentioned as follows,

> *"Noon. By the Pen and what they write. By the grace of Your Lord, you are not at all insane. And surely for you is an endless reward; and indeed you are upon excellent manners."*
> – Surah Qalam, Verse 1-4

In other words, 'O My Beloved ﷺ, pay no attention to his rants, because I (Allah ﷻ) declare your excellence. Don't listen to him, but be attentive to the proclamations of your Lord.' Thereafter, this insolence became the target of Divine retribution. Allah ﷻ revealed ten faults of the wretch Waleed ibn Mugheera,

> *"But do not yield to any mean swearer, backbiter, going about with slander, forbidder of good, transgressor, sinful, ignoble, cruel, and after all that, of doubtful birth."*
> – Surah Qalam, Verse 10-13

When Waleed heard this verse, he went to his mother and said, "From the ten faults Muhammad has attributed to me, I accept nine of them because I know I possess these defects; but tell me, am I of legitimate or illegitimate birth? Tell me the truth or I'll slay your head!" She replied, "Yes, you are illegitimate. Your father was very wealthy but impotent. I feared others taking this money away from me since I had no children, so I called a certain shepherd and you are the result of him and I."

The above verse declares those who make disrespecting the Holy Prophet ﷺ their profession to be from an illegitimate source. Such foul-mouthed wretches should examine their genealogies. Allah ﷻ promised further on,

> "We will soon brand upon him the swine-like snout."
> – Surah Qalam, Verse 16

In other words, 'We will deface him by making his ugly inner-self become apparent from the outside.' Whatever Waleed will have to endure in the Hereafter will definitely be severe and harsh, but his face was deformed even in this world. – *Jalaalain, Khazaainul-Irfaan, etc.*

Even today, no *noor* emanates from the faces of those who slander Rasoolullah ﷺ. Some of these wretches even have flies squatting on their faces, and in the Hereafter, they will surely be abhorrently disfigured. We seek Allah's ﷻ protection from this.

2. Once, Abu Lahab made the following statement of rudeness to the Noble Messenger ﷺ, "May your hand be broken." Allah ﷻ replied in anger,

> "The hands of Abu Lahab have perished and he too has perished. His wealth and what he earned did not profit him. Soon will he enter a blazing fire; And as for his wife, the carrier of firewood, around her neck will be a rope of twisted fibre."
> – Surah Lahab, Verse 1-5

The miserable Abu Lahab uttered just one statement of disrespect, but you've just read how he and his wife Umme-Jamil were censored by Almighty Allah ﷻ in reply. Of course, the promise made in this Surah was fulfilled. Umme-Jamil used to carry loads of thorns on her head and throw them in the path of the Beloved Messenger ﷺ. One day, she was carrying a load for this very task when, out of tiredness, she sat on a rock. An angel then pulled back the load she was carrying and the rope used to fasten the thorns got stuck tightly around her neck. This was how she died.

Neither Waleed nor Abu Lahab remain in this world, but day and night, they are the targets of curses by those who recite the Quran, infamously remembered with these attributes mentioned by Allah ﷻ Himself.

The grand court of the Prophet ﷺ is not seen by physical eyes anymore, his waleemah is not present and the sweet voice of the Beloved ﷺ is not heard. It was not our good fortune to physically see the splendour of his gatherings and hear his blessed voice, but still, the respect and etiquette of these blessed assemblies are still enjoined amongst people. If generations of latter times weren't fortunate enough to see these sights, at least they can bring Imaan after hearing about them. How beautifully did Dr. Iqbal observe and state,

> 'There is a place of respect beneath the sky more fragile than the Arsh. The likes of even Junaid ؓ and Bā-Yazīd ؓ come and lose themselves in it (i.e. the Prophet's ﷺ court).'

Oath on Allah ﷻ! Whoever is damned and cursed in this court will not find any protection anywhere. A criminal in the sight of a king is saved from his retribution after death, but an insulter to the Prophet ﷺ will not find peace even in his grave. However, one who is beloved by him will find peace everywhere.

There was a person who used to be a Scribe of Revelation. In time, he was unfortunate to have reverted back to Christianity and began to speak insolently against the Messenger ﷺ. After he died and was buried, the earth he was placed in spat him out! Thinking that the Sahaabah had unearthed him, his friends then dug a deeper grave than the first and buried him again. However, the earth *still* didn't take him in and spat him out once more. In short, he was buried several times but his corpse was never accepted. *When someone is rejected in the Prophet's ﷺ court, where will he ever find acceptance?*

It's recorded in *Madaarijun-Nubuwwah* that two daughters of the Holy Prophet ﷺ, Sayyidah Ruqaiyah ؓ and Sayyidah Umme-Kulthum ؓ, were both married to two of Abu Lahab's sons, Utba and Ateeba. They were in their nikah because nikah with polytheists was not prohibited yet. When Surah Lahab was revealed, Abu Lahab said to his sons, "Divorce the daughters of Muhammad, and if you don't, I'll disown you from my inheritance." So, Ateeba came to the Prophet ﷺ, respectfully apologized and gave talaaq (divorce). Utba, on the other hand, very disrespectfully gave talaaq, which caused the Prophet ﷺ to supplicate, "O Allah ﷻ, appoint a dog to meet out punishment to him." When Utba heard this, he became scared, rushed to his father and informed him of the supplication. Abu Lahab replied, "My son is now bereft of goodness since Muhammad's curse has fallen upon him." The father of Flames (Abu Lahab) then began to watch over his son in every possible manner. This was the very Utba who went to Syria as the leader of a trading caravan. One night, they stopped to rest at a particular place and a lion appeared from a nearby bush. It began to smell each person's mouth but left everyone unharmed. However, when it smelt the mouth of Utba it tore him apart! We can ascertain from this that a foul stench is emitted by one who is disrespectful to the Holy Prophet ﷺ. Even when animals smell this stench, they come to know why it's there.

Now, read about the condition of those who are all beloveds in the Noble Messenger's ﷺ court: Hadrat Safeena ؓ (the freed slave of Rasoolullah ﷺ) was once captured by the Kuffaar, but after a few days, he received news that a Muslim army had come to that particular area. At night, he managed to escape, but while he was running, he came across a lion and said to it, "I'm the slave of the Prophet ﷺ and I've lost my way." Hearing this, the lion stepped in front of him wagging its tail and showed him the path back, staying with the Companion all the way until he rejoined the Muslim army. - *Mishkaat, Baabul-Karaamaat*

These few incidents are sufficient for Muslims to ponder over. It's necessary for believers to profess the greatness of the Prophet ﷺ and teach our children his excellences, and the duty of the Islamic scholars is to disseminate knowledge of this topic to them. Never doubt the fact that the knowledge of Islam lies in the greatness of Rasoolullah ﷺ, since a home's admiration is caused by those who live within it. An example to show this is as follows. Consider a Hindu, Jew, Christian and Muslim gathering together for a meeting. The Hindu stands up and says, "My Raam is so powerful that he broke a heavy bow into two pieces to marry Seeta." The Christian says, "Jesus (Hadrat Esa ؑ) is so glorified that he gave life back to the dead and made them profess their faith to him." The Jew says, "The glory of Moses (Hadrat Musa ؑ) is that he made fountains of water gush forth from a stone that he struck with his staff." Now, if a Muslim stands up and says what some recent insolent 'Aalims' such as Maulwi Ismail Dehlwi and Maulwi Khalil Ambethwi have written (that 'My prophet is a helpless servant who doesn't know what's behind a wall; is more insignificant than a speck of dust, has knowledge less than the angel of death and Shaitaan,' etc.), then tell me, would this Muslim have honored Islam or caused it disgrace? If the Muslim said this to the followers of other religions, they'd say, "Our salutations from afar go to such an Islam whose leader's helplessness is so pitiful."

Yes, if a humble slave like me was present in such a gathering, I'd passionately proclaim, "O Hindu, if your Raam broke a heavy bow into two pieces, marvel at the Divinely bestowed strength of my Prophet ﷺ, that just by the mere gesture of his finger, he split the entire moon in two." I'd say to the Christian, "If Hadrat Esa عليه السلام gave life back to the dead, then indeed my Beloved's ﷺ power is such that he made lifeless and dry sticks, trees of jungles, and even *stones* recite his Kalima," and I'd say to the Jew, "If Hadrat Musa عليه السلام extracted water from a stone, how great is my Prophet ﷺ, who caused fountains of water to emerge from his blessed fingers?"

In short, to show the glory of Islam, it's absolutely pivotal and necessary to demonstrate the grandeur of Islam's founder and prophet, Muhammad Mustapha ﷺ. It's unfortunate that some Muslim-like apostates of this era cannot comprehend this secret. Shaitaan is whispering to them that proclaiming the greatness of all Prophets عليهم السلام is tantamount to disrespecting Allah ﷻ. These fools have understood their devilish monotheism to be Islam's spirit for the oneness of Allah ﷻ, and that to disrespect the Prophet ﷺ is actually a reflection of Allah's ﷻ power. The ability of a student establishes the prowess of a teacher. Likewise, the splendor of an object demonstrates the excellence of its maker. So, when thinking about the Messenger's ﷺ greatness, we will have to ultimately state, "O My Beloved Nabi ﷺ, how unrivalled is your Lord's power for it to make such an entity of excellence like you?!"

Keeping this in mind, this beggar (Mufti Ahmed Yaar Khan رحمه الله) has written two books, *Shaan'e-Habibur-Rahman* and *Jā'al-Haqq*.[1] Through the grace of Allah ﷻ, I would never have even hoped of the acceptance they have attained. The Ahle-Sunnah have written letters of dua and appreciation for these books, and no Wahabi or Deobandi scholar has had the courage to object to them. Instead, through the mercy of Allah ﷻ, many Deobandis have even repented from Wahabism and have embraced true Sunni Islam after reading them.

However, some Sunnis have insisted that three more contentious issues of this era be discussed, some of which were covered in *Jā'al-Haqq*. Amongst them is the topic of the Prophet's ﷺ authority and dominion. Deobandis and Wahabies refute this and attempt to show the helplessness of the prophets by using verses of the Quran which were in actual fact referring to helpless idols. Even verses revealed for idol-worshippers are used by them in rebuttals against Muslims. Scholars of this sort can only see one verse in the Quran,

'(O Beloved Prophet ﷺ), Say, "I am a man like you."
– Surah Kahf, Verse 110

In trust of Allah ﷻ, I have penned this topic but know that this and other work is not from my ability and power; it is the Beloved ﷺ who engages his service from whoever he wishes.

The name of this book is *Sultanat-e-Mustapha* ﷺ *dar Mumlikat-e-Kibriyaa*, and it is in the style of *Jā'al-Haqq*. This issue will be discussed in two chapters, the first proving the kingship of the Holy Prophet ﷺ, and the second containing objections of refuters and their answers.

Ahmed Yaar Khan Naeemi Ashrafi
Chancellor of Madrassah Ghousia Naeemia
Gujrat, Punjab
22nd Zil-Qadah 1362 AH, Monday

---

[1] *Contact Islamic Lifestyle Solutions for information on the English translations of these works.*

INTRODUCTION

Through the command of Allah ﷻ, the Holy Prophet Muhammad Mustapha ﷺ is the *maalik* (king), master and *mukhtaar* (one with authority & choice) of both the world and the Hereafter. He is the king of space and time, the Heavens, the Earth, and by the bestowal of Allah ﷻ, the master of Allah's ﷻ commands and bounties.

> 'The Creator has made you (O Rasoolullah ﷺ)
> the master of everything. Both the worlds are within
> your control and power.'

O Prophet of Allah ﷺ, you bestow to whoever you wish from your Lord's bounties and keep distant from them whatever you wish. You make Halaal for whoever you wish and Haraam for whoever you wish. In short, you are the king and master of both worlds. Alahazrat Imam Ahmed Raza ؓ states,

> 'Your command is legally valid. Authority belongs to you, whether it be the might of the sword or the power of the pen. You can do whatever you wish within a moment, because, O Master, it is your domain and reign.'

By the grace of Allah ﷻ, the Ahle-Sunnat wal-Jamaat become ecstatic when hearing this, and their Imaan strengthens as a result. However, not Hindus, Christians or other non-Muslims, but people who unfortunately claim to be Muslims (i.e. Wahabies, Deobandies) became enraged and burn up in anger. A simple question is then posed to them, "When Allah ﷻ is the giver and His Beloved ﷺ is the taker [of these qualities], why do you become angry?"

We will ask Allah ﷻ how much and what exactly did He bestow His Beloved Prophet ﷺ with, and then ask the Prophet ﷺ how much and what exactly did he take from Him. Then, we will enquire from the Sahaabah & the Ummah regarding their beliefs on the matter and will finally complete the chapter with rational proofs. Objections by those who refute these beliefs will then be answered in the second chapter.

Therefore, the first chapter will be divided into four sections,

1. Quranic verses proving the kingship of the Prophet ﷺ.
2. Ahadith on the same matter.

3. Verdicts and opinions of the Commentators of Quran, Hadith and other famous Scholars.

4. Rational proofs.

The Holy Prophet ﷺ being the master of both worlds doesn't mean that Allah ﷻ has no authority over them. It also doesn't mean that the prophet is a 'king' in the same sense as Allah ﷻ and that both are equal. Rather, the dominion of Allah ﷻ is true and eternally existent (Haqeeqi, Qadeem, Azali & Abadi) while the kingship of the Messenger ﷺ is bestowed and non-eternal (Ataa'i & Haadith), the way a king of this world is the owner of his dominion, how we are the masters and owners of our homes and possessions, and how Hadrat Sulaiman عليه السلام was the master of the world. This doesn't mean that Allah ﷻ isn't the king of these things at any time, but that He is the true (Haqeeqi) king and we are the figurative ones. His domain is eternal and ours is bestowed. This is the likeness of the Prophet's ﷺ dominion when compared to Allah's ﷻ.

Chapter One

Section One – Quranic Verses

'This revenge of theirs was (their) only return for the bounty with which Allah ﷻ and His Messenger ﷺ had enriched them out of his grace!'
– Surah Tauba, Verse 74

This verse proves that the Holy Prophet ﷺ makes people wealthy, because only he who's himself the owner can give to others. It's also apparent that the personal pronoun in 'his grace' refers to 'Rasool' ﷺ (because it's the closest to it).

'And if they had been pleased with what Allah ﷻ and His Messenger ﷺ had given them and would have said, "Sufficient for us is Allah ﷻ. Allah ﷻ and His Messenger ﷺ will give us of His bounty. To Allah ﷻ do we turn in submission."'
– Surah Tauba, Verse 59

It's established from this that the Prophet ﷺ does bestow and will bestow in future. Only he who has something himself can be the giver. If it's asked, "What does he give?" then the answer would be, "Whatever Allah ﷻ gives," because in this verse, a singular act of giving has been related to two.

'O Beloved ﷺ, We have granted you the Kauthar.'
– Surah Kauthar, Verse 1

'Kauthar' here may refer to the Fountain of Kauthar, copious goodness, an extensive Ummah, the Station of Praise (Maqaam-e-Mahmood), the greatest rank as intercessor, an extensive amount of prophetic miracles, worldly dominion, the conquering of empires or greatness over the entire creation. Whatever it is, we come to know that Allah ﷻ granted a great deal, and the Beloved ﷺ took all that was given. 'We gave' is a verb in the past tense, proving that this transaction has already been made and that control has already been given.

All the blessings of the world have been classified as *qaleel* by Allah ﷻ, meaning 'very little', but whatever Rasoolullah ﷺ was given is described as *katheer* ('much') or *akhtar* ('most'). In fact, in this verse, it is said to be *kauthar*, meaning not just more, but *the greatest possible amount*. **Even a** hundredth of the world is nothing compared to what has been given to our Beloved ﷺ.

> *"(O Beloved ﷺ) Undoubtedly, We have granted you a clear victory."*
> – Surah Fath, Verse 1

This verse proves that Allah ﷻ gave the Holy Prophet ﷺ *fat'h* (victory). If fat'h is meant here as the conquering of countries, it's apparent that the conqueror is the king of the conquered land, thus establishing the Prophet's ﷺ kingship.

If it refers to another of its possible meanings: i.e. 'to open', the verse would mean, "O Beloved ﷺ, We have opened for you closed doors." And so we conclude that the doors which were closed for others were opened for the Noble Messenger ﷺ, including the door of Jannah, intercession and every blessing.

> *'And (O Beloved ﷺ), He (Allah ﷻ) found you needy so He enriched you."*
> – Surah Duhaa, Verse 8

> *"And soon your Lord will give you (O Beloved ﷺ) so much that you will be well pleased."*
> – Surah Duhaa, Verse 5

Both of these verses prove that Allah ﷻ bestowed Rasoolullah ﷺ with so much that he became free from both worlds. When Allah ﷻ has already given and the Holy Prophet ﷺ has already taken, his dominion and power is definitely proven.

> *'And great is the grace of Allah ﷻ upon you.'*
> – Surah Nisaa, Verse 113

It's customary to say about a wealthy person, "Allah's ﷻ favour is great upon him." In this spirit, Allah ﷻ says to the Holy Prophet ﷺ, "Great is the grace of Allah ﷻ upon you." Bear in mind that the *entire world* has been termed as 'little' by Allah ﷻ in the Holy Quran (in fact, the literal meaning of *dunya* is 'insignificant'). What can now be the kingship of the Holy Prophet ﷺ when the word 'great' was used to describe what was bestowed to him?!

Even Hadrat Sulaiman ﷺ was bestowed kingship over the entire world, but Allah ﷻ didn't say to him, "Allah's ﷻ grace is great upon you." We can deduce that the throne, crown and dominion of Hadrat Sulaiman ﷺ was only a portion of territory within the domain of our Beloved Prophet ﷺ.

> *"(O Beloved ﷺ), accept the sadaqah out of their wealth to purify and clean them. And pray for them. Undoubtedly, your prayer is a solace for their hearts."*
> – Surah Tauba, Verse 103

In this verse, the Noble Messenger ﷺ is given two commands,

1. 'Whatever sadaqah the Companions present from their wealth in your court out of repentance, purify them by accepting it.'

2. 'Also, make dua for them.'

We can ascertain the following from this,

- That specific sadaqah, which is an act of worship, is only worthy of acceptance when the Holy Prophet ﷺ accepts it. If this wasn't the case, the Sahaabah would've given it to anyone.

- No one can become purified by worship alone. Rather, purity is attained by the mercy of the Prophet ﷺ, as the verse states, "And purify them."

- Without the intercession of Rasoolullah ﷺ, Allah ﷻ doesn't bestow anyone with anything. The verse states, "Make dua for them." Even though it is within the power of Allah ﷻ to give them everything, He still chooses not to until His Beloved ﷺ asks first.

- The Companions were not satisfied with their deeds until they were acknowledged by the Holy Prophet ﷺ. The verse states, "Your prayer is a solace for their hearts."

Alahazrat Imam Ahmed Raza ﷺ states,

> *'Will Allah ﷻ grant without his (the Prophet's ﷺ) means? Definitely not. This is wrong, and the false notion of those without vision.'*

> *'And he forbids them from unclean things.'*
> – Surah Aaraaf, Verse 157

> '(And the Kuffaar) do not forbid what Allah ﷻ and His Messenger ﷺ have made Haraam.'
> – Surah Tauba, Verse 29

Both of these verses prove that the Prophet ﷺ has the power and right to make things Haraam (i.e. the power of prohibition). From this, we can understand that he is also the master of rulings & commands. The prohibition of consuming dogs, donkeys, cats, etc. is not found in the Holy Quran; it's found in the Hadith.

> 'And it's not befitting for a Muslim man and a Muslim woman, when Allah ﷻ and His Messenger ﷺ have decreed something, that they should have any choice in their matters.'
> – Surah Ahzaab, Verse 36

The background of the revelation of this verse is as follows: The Prophet ﷺ once sent a proposal of nikah for Hadrat Zaid ibn Haaritha ؓ (a freed slave who used to be in his service) to Sayyidah Zainab bint Jahsh ؓ, a highly respected and noble lady of the Quraish. She and her brother, Abdullah ibn Jahsh, chose not to accept the proposal because she was a respected Quraishi, and so marrying Hadrat Zaid ؓ would be against *kufu* (compatibility). The above verse was then revealed and all parties had to agree. Thereafter, the nikah was made.

We can deduce from this that the Prophet ﷺ is the *maalik* (owner) of the lives, wealth and children of the Muslims; and such a king that no one even has a choice over his life, wealth or children against his command. In nikah, the permission of a mature female and the consent of her family members is definitely taken into account. In this nikah, however, the dissatisfaction of Sayyidah Zainub ؓ was not considered since all Muslim males and females are the slaves of Rasoolullah ﷺ, and the master has the right to make the nikah of his female slave with whom he wishes.

> "(O Beloved ﷺ), Say, "O my servants who have committed excesses against their own souls, do not despair of the mercy of Allah ﷻ."
> – Surah Zumr, Verse 53

In this verse, the Holy Prophet ﷺ has been permitted to call and regard all Muslims as his slaves. Only he who is the owner and king of all can call everyone his slaves.

> "O Believers, respond to the call of Allah ﷻ and the Messenger ﷺ when the Messenger ﷺ calls you."
> – Surah Anfaal, Verse 24

Obeying the Holy Prophet ﷺ and responding promptly to his call is necessary on Muslims no matter what state they are in, because obedience to the master is compulsory.

In summary, the mind cannot comprehend the greatness of the Holy Prophet's ﷺ dominion and glory. On his advent, time experienced a revolution, the world changed, and even Allah ﷻ adjusted the rules of His kingdom. Before this, Allah ﷻ would demonstrate to the world His omnipotence and the nature of His power, but after the advent of the Prophet ﷺ, He displayed His nature of compassion and protection. The previous nations were punished after committing just a single sin, some were humiliatingly disfigured, stones rained down on them, heavy floods destroyed them, and people were even changed into monkeys and swine, etc. However, when the disbelievers of Makkah said, "O Allah ﷻ, if Islam is true, make stones rain upon us," the answer to their supplication was not this nor any other punishment, but the following,

> "And it is not the work of Allah ﷻ to give them punishment while you are with them."
> – Surah Anfal, Verse 33

Subhanallah! The non-Muslims were worthy of punishment befalling them, but out of regard for the Mercy unto Creation, Allah ﷻ left them alone. Even if we reflect on our current state, we see that today we commit every sin that previous nations were punished for, yet no punishment befalls us. This is the blessing of Sayyiduna Rasoolullah ﷺ, the master of both worlds, that there is peace on the Earth.

اللهم صلى على سيدنا محمد و على آله و صحبه اجمعين

Section Two – Ahadith

1. The Holy Prophet ﷺ said, "The keys to the treasures of the earth were brought and handed to me." - *Mishkaat, Baabu Fadhaaili Sayyidil-Mursaleen*

Allah ﷻ granted the Holy Prophet ﷺ the keys to all of the treasures of the earth, and a 'key' is only given to an owner. Think for a moment, what exactly does 'treasures of the earth' entail? Mankind, animals, every type of grain & fruit, gold, silver, pearls, rubies, emeralds, precious gems, etc. are all treasures, and the Holy Prophet ﷺ is the master of all of them.

2. He also said,

"I've been granted two treasures, one red and the other white."
– *Ibid*

The Noble Messenger ﷺ has been granted all gold & silver, and has been given control over them too so that his *milkiyyat* (ownership) over them is established.

3. The Prophet ﷺ states,

"If I wish so, many mountains of gold can travel with me."
– *Mishkaat, Baabu Akhlaaqin-Nabi* ﷺ

The Prophet ﷺ is the owner & controller (maalik & mukhtaar) in every way, even if he doesn't wish to demonstrate it.

4.
"Verily I am the distributor and Allah ﷻ is the giver."
– *Mishkaat, Kitaabul-Ilm*

Whatever is given by Allah ﷻ is received by that person through the distribution of the Holy Prophet ﷺ entirely. In this Hadith, there's no restriction of time or object on Allah's ﷻ giving and the Prophet's ﷺ distributing. Now, what does the Holy Prophet ﷺ distribute? He distributes whatever Allah ﷻ gives, and Allah ﷻ is the Giver of everything. Only He who is the true Owner (i.e. Allah ﷻ) has given everything to can distribute everything himself. So, the control and dominion of the Holy Prophet ﷺ is proven here too.

5. Once, out of satisfaction with Hadrat Rabia ibn Ka'ab Aslami ؓ, the Holy Prophet ﷺ said to him, "Ask for something." He replied, "(O Rasoolullah ﷺ), I ask you for your companionship in Jannah." The Messenger ﷺ then asked, "Do you wish for anything else?" but the Companion simply replied that that was the only thing he desired. – *Mishkaat, Baabus-Sujood wa Fadhlihi*

This Hadith proves the kingship of the Prophet ﷺ by way of the following,

a. The Prophet ﷺ said, "Ask for something," with no restriction. Only someone who has everything in his control can say this. Hadrat Rabia ؓ thought well and asked for something unrivalled (i.e. Jannah at the greatest height, next to the Holy Prophet ﷺ).

b. Hadrat Rabia ؓ said, "I ask you…" He didn't say, "I ask Allah ﷻ…" In turn, the Prophet ﷺ didn't reply, "You are now a polytheist for making me a partner to Allah ﷻ." We know that only the owner of a particular thing is asked for it. So, the Prophet ﷺ being the king of Jannah is proven here too.

c. The Prophet ﷺ also asked him, "Do you ask for anything else?" proving that he is powerful enough to bestow other things besides Jannah. However, Hadrat Rabia ؓ thought to himself, "When I have Rasoolullah ﷺ, what else do I need?" and therefore chose not to ask for anything else (even though the benevolence of the Prophet ﷺ would have never refused him if he did).

Alahazrat Imam Ahmed Raza ؓ states,

> '*He who gives does so with limits.*
> *Verily the best giver is our Beloved Nabi ﷺ.*'

6. Hadrat Jabir ؓ had a little flour and meat at home which the Holy Prophet ﷺ placed his blessed saliva onto, causing them both to suffice for hundreds of people. Even after they ate, the flour and meat didn't lesson, and the womenfolk who prepared the bread from the flour felt no tiredness while preparing it. – *Mishkaat, Baabul-Mu'jizaat*

7. During a battle, the Prophet ﷺ placed his blessed hand in a bowl and caused fountains of water to gush forth from his blessed fingers. One

hundred and fifty people then drank this water and even used it for wudhu. – *Ibid*

8. The well of Hudaibiyah had a little water in it until Rasoolullah ﷺ placed an arrow inside it and caused the water to increase. – *Ibid*

9. The Prophet ﷺ also called an old lady once and opened the cap of her water-bag for his Companions. The water was sufficient for all of them, and they even filled their own water-bags from it. Even after all of this, it didn't lessen one bit. – *Ibid*

We can deduce the following from these narrations with regards to the Prophet ﷺ being the owner of everything,

a. The Holy Prophet ﷺ took guests with him to a meal on the invitation of Hadrat Jabir ؓ without the host's permission and made people drink the water of the old lady without her consent. However, people cannot take uninvited guests to the home they are invited to without the permission of the owner, and neither can someone else's possessions be shared without the owner's consent. We can therefore declare that the Holy Prophet ﷺ is the owner of everyone and everyone is his slave.

b. Think for a moment, where was the water from the water-bag, well and fingers coming from? The answer is that at that moment, connection to the Fountain of Kauthar and Salsabīl was made and their water was given to all. That's why the water from the Prophet's ﷺ blessed fingers has been regarded as more excellent than the water of Zum-Zum.

10. The Holy Prophet ﷺ said,

> "In this Salaatul-Khusoof (Salaah on a lunar eclipse), I saw Jannah and I held a bunch of grapes from it. If I had broken the branch, you would've eaten from it until Qiyaamat."
> – Mishkaat, Baabu Salaatil-Khusoof

The Holy Prophet ﷺ was permitted to break the grapes of Jannah while standing in Madina Sharif and even give his Companions to eat. Though he chose not to, it still proves that he is the owner of everything in Jannah even while in this world.

11. Once, Rasoolullah ﷺ intended to make istinja in a field which had two trees very far apart from one another. For the purpose of privacy, he took hold of the trees and brought them together, and the trees followed him like camels. He then relieved himself while covered by them. – *Mishkaat, Baabul-Mu'jizaat*

12. It is stated that the dead regained life and brought conviction on Islam at the hands of Rasoolullah ﷺ. He even brought his father and mother (Sayyidah Amina ؓ and Hadrat Abdullah ؓ) back to life and made them Muslims. – *Shaami, Baabul-Murtaddeen*

13. *Shaami* also states in the same juncture that Hadrat Ali ؓ sacrificed his Asr Salaah for the resting of the Holy Prophet ﷺ. The incident is as follows: After having performed his Asr Salaah, the Prophet ﷺ placed his blessed head on the lap of Hadrat Ali ؓ and fell asleep. The Companion had not performed his Asr yet, but he chose to continue sitting while the sun set, knowing that if he stood up for Salaah, the sleep of the Prophet ﷺ would have been disrupted. The sun eventually set and Hadrat Ali's ؓ Asr became qadhaa. When the Prophet ﷺ awoke, he brought back the set sun and allowed Hadrat Ali ؓ to perform his Asr Salaah in the right time.

Both of these narrations show that Rasoolullah ﷺ is the king of both worlds. The Imaan of a person is not acceptable after his or her death, and when the time of Salaah has passed, the prayer cannot be anything but qadhaa. But how magnificent is the dominion of this king that he gave his parents Imaan after their demise and even made them Companions, all accepted by Allah ﷻ? He also returned a qadhaa Salaah back to its original time! (Those who had previously performed their Asr were not commanded to redo their prayer. This was for Hadrat Ali ؓ only).

14. During Jumaa, at the time of the khutba, a Companion once complained about drought to the Holy Prophet ﷺ while he was on the mimbar. After Rasoolullah ﷺ made dua for rain, it began to pour before the khutba could even end, and it rained continuously until the following Jumaa, when the same Companion complained that the rain was now excessive and that the foundations of their homes were giving way due to it. Standing on the mimbar, the Messenger ﷺ then gestured with his two fingers to the clouds and caused them to sway away in delight. Rasoolullah ﷺ then said, "O Allah ﷻ, make it rain around us, not over us." And that is exactly what happened. – *Mishkaat, Baabul-Mu'jizaat*

We see here that Rasoolullah ﷺ has dominion over the clouds, because **they moved on his gesture.** Their coming and going is not based on any season or climate.

15. The Holy Prophet ﷺ once rode the stubborn horse of Hadrat Abu Talha ؓ, after which it became tame and never showed stubbornness from then on. – *Ibid*

16. The Prophet ﷺ once ordered a person who was eating with his left hand to eat with his right. The man arrogantly replied, "My right hand is useless." The Prophet ﷺ then said, "It's useless from today." The man's hand then went dead and he couldn't even lift it to his mouth! – *Ibid*

We ascertain that the movement and power of a human body part are both under the command of the Prophet ﷺ.

17. Clouds used to shade the Prophet ﷺ: the monk Buhaira once invited Rasoolullah ﷺ for a meal, and the invitation was held under a tree. Due to the great number of people that attended, the shade was already taken up, but when the Noble Messenger ﷺ arrived, the tree itself bent down to shade him! – *Ibid*

When standing in the sun, the kings of this world are shaded by the umbrellas their servants carry. Marvel at the kingship of the Beloved ﷺ, however, that even clouds and trees know that he is their master! So, they are both obliged and happy to serve him.

18. The Messenger ﷺ once touched a weak goat and milked it. With only a small amount, the milk was sufficient for an entire congregation. – *Ibid*

19. Rasoolullah ﷺ once set foot in the orchard of Hadrat Anas ؓ, and due to the blessings of his entry, the orchard gave fruits twice in one year! – *Mishkaat, Baabul-Karaamaat*

20. Hadrat Abu Hurairah ؓ states,

"Hadrat Uthman ibn Affaan ؓ bought Jannah twice from the Holy Prophet ﷺ. The first when there was no other well in Madina besides the well of Rooma. Hadrat Uthman ؓ purchased it and donated it. The second was on the occasion of the Battle of Tabuk, when

the Muslim soldiers had no weapons or provisions. Hadrat Uthman ؓ bought what was required and gave it to them.
– *Haakim, Ibn Adi, Ibn Asaakir*

Hadrat Uthman ؓ purchased Jannah from Rasoolullah ﷺ in exchange for the well of Rooma. The Prophet ﷺ sold it, and only he who is the owner can sell something.

21. Hadrat Jaabir ؓ narrates that the Noble Messenger ﷺ said, "I have been given the keys of this world; Jibrael ؑ brought them to me on a spotted horse." – *Ahmed, Abu Nuaim, Ibn Hibban*

22. Ibn Abbas ؓ narrates from the mother of the Prophet ﷺ, Sayyidah Amina ؓ, "When [Muhammad ﷺ] was born, he went into sajda. A white cloud then took him from me, disappeared, and then appeared again after a short while. I saw that my son now had keys in his blessed hands, and someone was proclaiming, "The Prophet ﷺ has taken control over the keys of victory & prophethood." Thereafter, another cloud approached me and again took him from me. When it reappeared, someone was saying,

"Good, good. He has taken control over the entire world. There is no creation in the world who does not fall under his dominion."
– *Abu Nuaim*

This extract has been supported by the narration of Mishkaat, with reference to Bukhari, which we presented in the beginning of this section. The verse,

انا فتحنا لك فتح مبينا
– Surah Fath, Verse 1

also corroborates it. It's clearly evident from this Hadith that the entire creation of Allah ﷻ falls under the kingship of the Beloved Prophet ﷺ. There are several others besides these that can be produced, but this much is sufficient for those with Imaan.

All of the above Ahadith establish that the Prophet ﷺ has kingship over the objects and creation of this world. We now present those Ahadith which prove that he is the controller of *commands*, can make whatever he desires Halaal, and can change the Quranic commands for whoever he wishes.

23. Once, the Holy Prophet ﷺ proclaimed, "O People, Hajj has been made fardh on you, so perform it." Someone asked, "O Rasoolullah ﷺ, is performing it fardh every year?" He replied, "If I say 'yes' now, it will be, and everyone will have to perform it annually." – *Mishkaat, Kitaabul-Hajj*

The utterances of the Holy Prophet ﷺ have a particular effect. Everyone is obliged by the commands of Allah ﷻ, but Divine instruction emits from the movement of His Beloved's ﷺ blessed lips. Whatever said by him will, in fact, become the command of Allah ﷻ.

24. The Holy Prophet ﷺ performed Taraweeh with Jama'at for a few nights and then stopped, saying, "If I continuously perform it, I fear it becoming fardh upon you, and you'll find it difficult to complete." – *Mishkaat, Baabu Qiyaami Shahri Ramadaan*

The practice of Rasoolullah ﷺ also becomes the command of Allah ﷻ.

25. A slave-woman once submitted to the Holy Prophet ﷺ, "I made a vow that if Allah ﷻ brings you safely from the battle, I'll play the duff before you and sing." The Prophet ﷺ replied, "Fine. Complete it." The woman then played the duff. – *Mishkaat, Baabul-Manaaqib*

26. A Hadith which is sound (Sahih) on the condition of Muslim is as follows,

"A person once came to the Prophet ﷺ and said that he will bring Imaan on condition that he performs only two Salaah. The Prophet ﷺ accepted this condition of his."
– *Musnad Imam Ahmad ibn Hambal* ﷺ

There are five Salaah compulsory on Muslims, but the Holy Prophet ﷺ excused this particular person from three. (Extracted from *Al-Amn wal-Ulaa* by Imam Ahmed Raza ﷺ).

We again come to know that the Noble Messenger ﷺ is the owner of commands.

27. Hadrat Ali ﷺ intended to make another nikah but the Prophet ﷺ said, "Ali ﷺ doesn't have permission to do so. Yes, if he wants to make another nikah, he should divorce Fathima ﷺ and then make it." – *Mirqaat, Sharah Mishkaat, Baabu Manaaqibi Ahlil-Bait*

The Holy Quran states,

> "Marry those who seem good to you, two, three or four."
> – Surah Nisaa, Verse 3

It's permissible for a man to keep up to four wives in his nikah, but in the presence of Sayyidah Fathima Zahra ؓ, Hadrat Ali ؓ didn't have the choice of making another nikah.

At the same juncture, Mirqaat states,

> "Causing distress to the Prophet ﷺ is Haraam even if something Halaal was acted upon. This is one of his unique qualities."

Mirqaat also states that making another nikah was Haraam for Hadrat Ali ؓ.

28. The Messenger ﷺ once left to a certain place to reconcile fighting Muslims while back home the time of Salaah had come, so Hadrat Bilal ؓ gave the Azaan and then went to Hadrat Abu Bakr Siddique ؓ saying, "Please lead the Salaah." So, the Salaah under the Imaamat of Hadrat Abu Bakr Siddique ؓ had already commenced when the return of the Holy Prophet ﷺ was announced. Hearing this, Hadrat Abu Bakr ؓ immediately stepped back as a *muqtadi* (follower) and the Holy Prophet ﷺ then became the Imam. – *Bukhari, Vol. 1, Kitaabus-Sulh*

Today, if a person comes while Salaah is being read, he must stand wherever he finds a place. How great then is our Beloved ﷺ, that he came while Salaah was in progress and it was immediately handed over to him, nullifying the Imaamat of the previous Imam? Without doubt, the Prophet ﷺ is the king of rulings and commands.

29. In a lengthy Hadith, the Holy Prophet ﷺ states, "Neither are we the inheritors of anyone nor do we have any inheritors." – *Bukhari, Vol. 1, Kitaabul-Jihad*

Although the Holy Quran commanding the distribution of inheritance is established, Rasoolullah ﷺ excluded himself from his. This prophetic proclamation was then acted upon by his Companions after his demise.

30. Rasoolullah ﷺ made the testimony of Hadrat Khuzaima Ansaari ؓ equal to two testimonies. – *Bukhari, Vol. 2, Kitaabut-Tafseer, Surah Ahzaab*

The incident is as follows: Rasoolullah ﷺ once purchased a horse from Sawaa ibn Haarith. Some time later, this Bedouin refused to acknowledge the sale and said, "I did not sell this horse to you. If you truly bought it from me, present a witness for your claim." It was the planning of Allah ﷻ that when this sale took place, no one else was present. Nevertheless, Hadrat Khuzaima ؓ submitted, "O Rasoolullah ﷺ, I bear witness that you bought this horse. You are true and the Bedouin is a liar." The Prophet ﷺ asked, "How can you bear witness? You didn't see the sale." Hadrat Khuzaima ؓ replied, "O Rasoolullah ﷺ, by hearing you, I have become witness to the Oneness of Allah ﷻ, the reality of Jannah, Jahannam, Qiyaamat and all other articles of faith. I recited the Kalima and gave testimony that Allah ﷻ has no partner. Is one horse greater than all of this? I bear witness simply by hearing you." This declaration of Hadrat Khuzaima ؓ was so accepted in the court of the Holy Prophet ﷺ that, from then on, his single testimony was made to equal two.

The Holy Quran states,

> "And call the witness, two just people from amongst you."
> – Surah Talaaq, Verse 2

However, when it came to Hadrat Khuzaima ؓ, his single testimony was accepted as the testimony of two, proving that the Holy Prophet ﷺ has the authority to exclude from the Holy Quran's command whoever he wishes.

31. Sayyidah Aisha ؓ submitted to the Prophet ﷺ,

> "I notice that your Lord hastens to fulfill your wish."
> – *Bukhari, Vol. 2, Kitaabut-Tafseer, Surah Ahzaab*

We come to know here that Allah ﷻ readily grants Rasoolullah's ﷺ desires the rank of being deeni (religious) commands.

32. The Holy Prophet ﷺ once permitted Umme-Atiyyah to make *nauha* (the beating of the chest, etc. on someone's death). – *Muslim Sharif*

He gave permission whereas making nauha is Haraam according to the Shariah.

33. Hadrat Ali ﷺ was given permission to give ghusl to Sayyidah Fathima ﷺ after her demise whereas a husband cannot give his deceased wife ghusl (because the nikah between them is broken by the woman's death). – *Shaami*

34. Hadrat Abu Bakr Siddique ﷺ was allowed to come into the musjid while in the state of *janaabat* (the state in which ghusl is obligatory upon a person) whereas it is impermissible for one to do so in this condition.

35. The Prophet ﷺ fed a Companion's sadaqah for the compensation of a fast to the Companion himself.

36. Once, the Holy Prophet ﷺ commanded, "Neither are the thorns of Makkah to be broken nor the game of the city interfered with." Hadrat Abbas ﷺ submitted, "O Rasoolullah ﷺ, allow us the Azkhar grass because it is used on the roofs of the houses, and blacksmiths burn it in their furnaces instead of coals." The Prophet ﷺ replied, "Fine, permission is granted for the Azkhar grass. It can be cut from the earth of Makkah." – *Muslim, Bukhari*

We come to know from this that the utterance of the Prophet ﷺ becomes the law of the Almighty ﷻ.

37. During the migration, the Holy Prophet ﷺ said to Hadrat Saraaqah ﷺ, "I see on your hand the gold bracelet of Kisra, the King of Persia." The result of this was that when Persia was conquered during the Caliphate of Hadrat Umar ﷺ, the bracelet of Kisra was given to Hadrat Saraaqah ﷺ to wear and remained with him from then on.

Wearing gold is Haraam for males, but was permitted here for Hadrat Saraaqah ﷺ.

38. Hadrat Ka'ab ibn Malik ﷺ once came under the rebuke of the Holy Prophet ﷺ, and his wives were commanded, "Don't let your husband come near you. No Muslim should meet or converse with him." – *Bukhari, Muslim, in the narration of Hadrat Ka'ab's ﷺ repentance*

During this period of boycott, the legitimate wives of Hadrat Ka'ab ﷺ became Haraam on him for a while due to the command of the Holy Prophet ﷺ. The Holy Quran states,

> *"Your wives are tilth for you, so approach your tilth at your will."*
> – Surah Baqarah, Verse 223

However, Hadrat Ka'ab ؓ was removed from this command at that time. Oath on Allah ﷻ, if this rebuke and prohibition had to last forever, the wives of Hadrat Ka'ab ؓ would've *remained* Haraam on him even though the nikah was lawful!

39. The Holy Prophet ﷺ once recited something and blew it (i.e. he made *dumm*) on the covering of Hadrat Abu Hurairah ؓ, who then kept the covering against his chest. The effect of this was that his memory increased dramatically. From then on, he never forgot anything, and this is why he narrated approximately 200,000 Ahadith. Strength of memory is the internal power of a human. However, Rasoolullah ﷺ has control over both a person's internal and external affairs. – *Mishkaat, Baabul-Mu'jizaat*

Section Three – Verdicts of the Islamic Scholars

The entire Ummah has always agreed that the Holy Prophet ﷺ is the king of both worlds. This is why the Sahaabah would ask Rasoolullah ﷺ for Jannah or complain to him about drought, etc. If someone did something wrong, he would even present himself in the court of the Prophet ﷺ to attain forgiveness. Once, a Companion committed a mistake within Shariah, so he came to the Prophet ﷺ and said,

> "O Messenger of Allah ﷺ, purify me."
> – Mishkaat, Baabul-Hudood

Sayyidah Aisha ؓ also states,

> "I make tauba to Allah ﷻ and His Rasool ﷺ."
> – Mishkaat, Baabut-Tasaaweer

In short, the Sahaaba would present themselves in the court of Rasoolullah ﷺ to remove every hardship and attain the mercy of Allah ﷻ. The Prophet ﷺ wouldn't say to them, "I'm helpless like you. Why do you ask me? If you want something, sit in the musjid and ask Allah ﷻ instead." On the contrary, he'd accept their request and fulfill their needs. The Sahaabah never presented themselves in this court out of their own accord. Rather, the Holy Quran itself instructed them (and the rest of creation) to go to the Prophet ﷺ when faced with hardship,

> "And if they do injustice unto their souls, then O Beloved ﷺ, they should come to you and beg forgiveness of Allah ﷻ, and the Messenger ﷺ should intercede for them. Then surely they would find Allah ﷻ most Relenting, Merciful."
> – Surah Nisaa, Verse 64

For a complete discussion on the abovementioned verse, refer to my books *Shaan-e-Habibur-Rahman* and *Jā'al-Haqq*. We, the mendicant, have been commanded to go to the Holy Prophet ﷺ and ask of him, while the Beloved Prophet ﷺ himself is instructed,

> "And do not censor the needy (i.e. bestow him and let him go)."
> – Surah Duhaa, Verse 10

The Sahaabah regarded the Noble Messenger ﷺ as the king, and similarly, after their era, the Ulama, Mashaaikh and general body of Muslims the world over also beseeched help from the Prophet ﷺ in their Qaseedas and Nasheeds. In their wazaaifs and amals, they formally sought the Prophet's ﷺ help and clearly state in their works that he is the king & owner (maalik). If the names of these personalities are listed, journals would be required. So, only a few will be presented as examples:

1. Under the annotation of the Hadith about Hadrat Rabia ibn Ka'ab Aslami ؓ, Shaikh Abdul-Haqq Muhaddith Dehlwi ؓ states, "We come to know that all affairs are in the hands of the Holy Prophet ﷺ. By the command of his Lord, he gives to whoever he wishes. If you desire the goodness of the world and the Hereafter, come to the court of Rasoolullah ﷺ and ask for whatever you wish." – *Ashiatul-Lam'aat Sharah Mishkaat, Baabus-Sujood*

2. In Mirqaat, Sharah Mishkaat, under the same Hadith, Mulla Ali Qaari ؓ states, "The Noble Messenger ﷺ gives to whoever he wishes."

These extracts have decided that the Prophet ﷺ is the king of every object of this world and the Hereafter. We should ask him for everything; honour, Imaan, Jannah, even the mercy of Allah ﷻ.

3. Under the verse, "And if they would have committed polytheism, surely all that they had already done would have been destroyed." – *Surah Anaam, Verse 88*

   Imaam Fakhruddin Raazi ؓ states, "Allah ﷻ has blessed the prophets with so much knowledge and *ma'rifat* (recognition) that they have dominion over the inner state of the creation and over their lives as well. They have been granted so much power that they have kingship over even the visible." – *Tafseer Kabeer*

The word '*khalq*' (creation) was used in this extract, referring to everything that is in the creation of Allah ﷻ, from the Heavens to the Earth. All is under the power of Rasoolullah ﷺ.

4. Allama Ibn Hajar Makki ؓ states, "Rasoolullah ﷺ is the greatest Khalifa of Allah ﷻ, as the treasures of the Almighty ﷻ and His blessings are in his hands and intentions. He gives to whoever he wishes. – *Al-Jawaahirul-Munazam, Pg. 52*

This establishes that all Divine treasures are in the control of the Beloved Messenger ﷺ.

5. Shaikh Abdul-Haqq Muhaddith Dehlwi ؓ writes, "The kingship of the Prophet ﷺ is on more than this. All angels, jinns, humans and the entire creation are under his control by the bestowal of Allah ﷻ." – *Ashiatul-Lam'aat, Vol. 1, Pg. 463*

6. Allama Yusuf ibn Ismail Nabhaani ؓ states, "The Holy Prophet ﷺ grants and prohibits, he fulfills the needs of the mendicant, removes the hardship of those who are struck by it, intercedes and enters into Jannah who he wishes. – *Shawaahidul-Haqq, Pg. 153*

The Prophet ﷺ is the fulfiller of needs and the remover of afflictions.

7. Imaam Qastalaani ؓ states, "May my mother and father be sacrificed on the king who had kingship from when Adam عليه السلام was between sand & water. When the Holy Prophet ﷺ desires something, nothing can occur contrary to his wish and no one can stop him." – *Mawaahibul-Ladunya, Vol. 1, Pg. 46*

We come to know from when the Prophet ﷺ was the king of the worlds, and that his every utterance is the key to reality.

8. He also writes, "Abul-Qaasim is one of the appellations of the Holy Prophet ﷺ because he allocates Jannah between its inmates." – *Mawaahibul-Ladunya, Vol. 1, Pg. 195*

9. Allama Taqiyuddin Subki ؓ states, "Without any similitude, understand Rasoolullah ﷺ to be the minister of the King, and that nothing reaches the King without going through the minister first." – *Shifaaus-Siqaam, Pg. 165*

This proves that the Prophet's ﷺ kingship is not only in this world but even in Jannah. Without him, no one will be able to attain any blessing of Paradise.

10. Imam Qastalaani ؓ states, "The Holy Prophet ﷺ is the treasury of tranquility; he is the point wherefrom a Divine command is emplaced, and no command is emplaced without coming from him." – *Mawaahibul-Ladunya, Vol. 1, Pg. 6*

The commands of Allah ﷻ are emplaced upon the world from the court of His Beloved ﷺ.

11. Shaikh Abdul-Haqq Muhaddith Dehlwi ؓ states, "The Noble Messenger ﷺ is the appointed judge and in-charge over (the affairs of) the Divine kingdom. All commands of the entire earth are in his custody. What greater kingship besides this is there? – *Ashiatul-Lam'aat, Vol. 1, Pg. 656*

The kingship of the Prophet ﷺ is the greatest kingship ever established. His rule is greater then even the kingships of Hadrat Sulaiman ؑ and Hadrat Zul-Qarnain ؓ.

12. Imam Busairi ؓ states, "The world and the hereafter is from the generosity of the Holy Prophet ﷺ. The knowledge of the Pen and the Tablet is only a part of his knowledge." – *Qaseeda Burda*

13. Imam Abu Hanifa Numaan ibn Thaabit ؓ states, "O Prophet of Allah ﷺ, I am aspirant of your benevolence. There is no one in the creation for Abu Hanifa ؓ besides you." – *Qaseeda Nu'maan*

14. Every Durood in *Dalaailul-Khairaat* is authentic and accepted by the entire Ummah. Saints and Scholars have always practiced its recital. In the Thursday section of the book, the following Durood appears, "O Allah ﷻ, send Durood on the Prophet ﷺ whose name is Muhammad ﷺ, his 'daal' (the last letter of the name) is the 'daal' of continuance, his 'haa' is the 'haa' of *rahmat* (mercy) and his 'meem' is the 'meem' of *milkiyyat* (dominion & power).

From the letters of the word 'Muhammad ﷺ', we come to know that he has always been the king of both worlds, and his kingship is one of mercy. The word 'Muhammad ﷺ' contains one 'haa', one 'daal' and two 'meem's. The two 'meems' refer to the possession of two dominions (i.e. the world and the Hereafter), the 'daal' is for *dawaam* (continuous, i.e. his kingship has been uninterrupted), and the 'haa' is for mercy (i.e. his kingship is one of mercy).

15. Maulana Jalaaluddin Rumi ؓ states, "The body of the Noble Messenger ﷺ remained on the Earth, but his blessed life is in the *Laa-Makaa*, which is further than the thought of the Saints. In fact, *Makaa* (space) and *Laa-Makaa* are both under his command and desire, just as how the four rivers of Jannah are for an inmate of Paradise. He (the Prophet ﷺ) remains in exclusive *me'raaj*

(ascension) at all times, and the Almighty places on his blessed head a special crown." – *Mathnawi Sharif*

Besides these, many other quotations can be presented, but we make do with the above.

The pious elders and the Sahaabah used to have the intention of making the Holy Prophet ﷺ pleased when completing Allah's ﷻ worship, proving that to intend keeping the Prophet ﷺ happy in one's worship is not for show or an act of polytheism. Rather, it is the soul of worship. In Section Two, you have read that while in the condition of Salaah, Hadrat Abu Bakr Siddique ؓ made Rasoolullah ﷺ the Imaam. The Salaah was for Allah ﷻ, but respect for the Holy Prophet ﷺ was made in it.

Under the verse,

> "And We gave Dawood ؈ the Zabur."
> – Surah Nisaa, Verse 163

Tafseer Khaazin and *Tafseer Roohul-Bayaan* contain the following Hadith. The Holy Prophet ﷺ once said to Hadrat Musa Ashari ؓ, "Tonight I heard your recitation of the Holy Quran. Allah ﷻ has granted you the 'Dawoodi' voice (i.e. the beautiful recital style of Hadrat Dawood ؈)." The Companion replied, "Oath on Allah ﷻ, if I knew that the Quran-personified (i.e. the Holy Prophet ﷺ) was listening to my recital, I would've recited with more arrangement."

Recitation of the Holy Quran is for Allah ﷻ, but even in this state, a Companion desired to make the Prophet ﷺ happy.

In the commentary of the verse,

> "My wage is only with Allah ﷻ and I have been ordered to be of the Muslims."
> – Surah Yunus, Verse 72

Tafseer Roohul-Bayaan states that Sayyidah Rabia ؓ used to perform 1,000 rakaats nafl daily and would say, "I don't desire their reward. I only hope that the Holy Prophet ﷺ is happy with me and will take pride in me on the Day of Qiyaamat, saying to the congregation of prophets, "Look, these are the deeds of a woman from my Ummah."

Subhanallah! Those with true love are indeed amazing!

Allah ﷻ also states,

> *"And for whoever goes forth from his home as an emigrant for Allah ﷻ and His Messenger ﷺ and death overtakes him, his reward lies with Allah ﷻ."*
> – Surah Nisaa, Verse 100

To migrate and leave one's homeland in the path of Allah ﷻ is worship, but it's necessary while migrating to please both Allah ﷻ and His Messenger ﷺ.

The Holy Quran states,

> *"It is more fitting that they should please Allah ﷻ and His Messenger ﷺ."*
> – Surah Tauba, Verse 62

We can deduce that to intend pleasing Allah ﷻ and the Holy Prophet ﷺ in performing a deed makes it worthier of acceptance. Doing so is not polytheism or Haraam. This is why making Salaam to the Prophet ﷺ is waajib in Salaah. His blessed name has also been added in the Kalima, the Azaan and many other forms of worship.

SECTION FOUR – RATIONAL PROOFS

1. The workings of this world are examples of the Hereafter. Refer to my book *Jā'al-Haqq* for a detailed explanation of this. A king makes his appointed governors the sub-rulers of his kingdom and grants them general power. Due to this bestowal, the governor says, "I can say this, I can do this." Thereafter, power runs according to rank. An ordinary soldier only has a certain amount of power, a captain has more than a soldier, a governor has more than a captain, a viceroy has power over the entire country, and the prime-minister has official power over the entire kingdom. With all this power, neither does the king's kingship diminish nor did any affair escape his control. Actually, the king was the true king and simply appointed others as temporary ones.

Similarly, Allah ﷻ made the Pen & Tablet a portion of His kingdom for the angels and chosen servants of the world. All the affairs and workings of the world are transcribed on the Tablet, and the angels and selected servants are to look at it and act accordingly. Due to this power, they can say, "I can do this."

The Holy Quran narrates the statement of Hadrat Esa ﷺ,

> "And I heal the blind and the leper and give life to the dead by the permission of Allah ﷻ."
> – Surah Aale-Imraan, Verse 49

And Hadrat Jibrael ﷺ said to Sayyidah Maryam ﷺ,

> "I have come to give you a pure son."
> – Surah Maryam, Verse 19

The Holy Quran states that the Holy Prophet ﷺ purifies the Muslims, teaches them the Book and Wisdom, and enriches the mendicant. Refer to the introduction of this book and *Jā'al-Haqq* for more on this. Ghouse-Azam Shaikh Abdul-Qadir Jilaani ﷺ states, "All the cities of Allah ﷻ are my property and under my dominion. Every month and moment which goes by in the world passes with my permission. (The reason for this is that) Every Saint is on the path of a particular prophet, and I am on the path treaded by Rasoolullah ﷺ."

In other words, "My secret lies at the blessed feet of the Noble Messenger ﷺ. Through its blessings, Allah ﷻ granted me honour."

In all of the above, did the glory of Allah ﷻ diminish in any way? Definitely not!

2. Everybody knows that near the time of one's demise, bringing Imaan when seeing the Angel of Death علیه السلام is not credible or accepted. Also, repentance can be made at any point in one's lifetime, but the doors of repentance close at the time of death.

However, the Holy Prophet ﷺ was granted the power to close the doors of repentance on whoever he wished, even during that person's lifetime. Thereafter, even if the person chose to repent, his or her repentance was not accepted. The Prophet ﷺ was also given the power to open the doors of repentance for whoever he wished and make them Muslims after bringing them back to life.

Rasoolullah ﷺ gave life back to his blessed parents after their demise and made them enter Islam (proof of this has already been presented). Celebrated scholars such as Imam Jalaaluddin Suyuti ؓ and Allama ibn Abidain Shaami ؓ have intensely researched this.

Only *once* did Tha'laba ibn Haatib refuse giving Zakaat. He later came with it but was denied its acceptance by the Prophet ﷺ. He then brought his Zakaat during the Caliphates of Hadrat Abu Bakr, Umar and Uthman ؓ but all declined it after giving the same reply, "We don't have the courage to accept the Zakaat which the Prophet ﷺ rejected." It was this very Tha'laba concerning whom the following Quranic verse was revealed,

> "And for them are some who promised Allah ﷻ
> that if He gives us out of His bounty, then we will surely
> give in charity and will surely become good people."
> – Surah Tauba, Verse 75

Refer to the commentary of this verse in *Tafseer Kabeer* and *Roohul-Bayaan*.

Tha'laba was still alive, the doors of repentance shouldn't have been closed for him, and if he repented, his tauba should've been accepted, but his doors of repentance were closed by Rasoolullah ﷺ. So, it wouldn't be accepted from him anymore.

3. Zakaat was not compulsory on the Holy Prophet ﷺ. - *Shaami, Kitaabuz-Zakaat*

   Why was this so? One of the reasons could be that all Muslims, males and females, are the slaves of the Holy Prophet ﷺ, and a master cannot give his slave Zakaat. Therefore, the Holy Prophet ﷺ couldn't give his Zakaat to anyone simply because there is no one to accept it. Zakaat was not made compulsory on him because a valid recipient of it is unfound.

4. The prophets are the Khalifas of Allah ﷻ.

   "Indeed I will make upon the earth a successor."
   – Surah Baqarah, Verse 30

   A Khalifa (viceroy) is someone who rules over the dominion of a king as his deputy. These prophets are the deputies of Allah ﷻ. The Almighty doesn't send commands to us directly. Rather, they are sent to and emplaced by the prophets. A deputy becomes the king of whatever land he is granted.

5. The Kalima 'Laa ilaaha Illalalaahu Muhammadur-Rasoolullah ﷺ' is written on the pillars of the Arsh, on the leaves of the trees of Jannah, on the foreheads of the Maidens and on the chests of the Ghilmaan. It is a rule that the name of the maker and master is written on their possession.

   We can understand from this that the Maker of Paradise and the Heavens is Allah ﷻ and their Master is Muhammadur-Rasoolullah ﷺ. Objects of this world also have the name of the Prophet ﷺ written on them (it is even written in the sky).

6. During the Me'raaj, the Prophet ﷺ was taken on a tour of the Heavens (and even beyond) because, sometimes, a king takes a tour of his kingdom. This was what happened on the night of Me'raaj.

7. Today, people criticize and speak negatively about the kings of this world, but no heart or tongue has the courage or power to speak against Rasoolullah ﷺ. If someone does display insolence to him, he

is punished; and there are numerous examples of this. We can deduce that this king even has dominion over the hearts and souls of people, and it will remain there until Qiyaamat. May Allah ﷻ make us his loyal subjects and save us from rebellion.

8. Worldly kings give salaries to their servants, and even today, thousands of people receive remuneration from the Holy Prophet's ﷺ court. I ask, what earthly-trade skill do the Islamic Scholars and Shuyookh have that their lives on this earth is so comfortable? Actually, these personalities are the slaves of the king of Madina, and so Muslims are their loyal servants simply because of this. O Allah ﷻ! You know that there is no other court besides Your Beloved's ﷺ for us.

O Wahabies and Deobandi scholars, be loyal to the court wherefrom you attain comfort in your lives. Don't search for faults in him, but proclaim his praise! May Allah ﷻ grant you salvation and keep us steadfast.

In fact, even Islamic organizations, councils and schools are all beggars of this court. They obtain charity from Muslims in the name of the Holy Prophet's ﷺ deen, and so it's necessary on them to promote Islamic teachings and conduct. Muslim politicians who obtain votes in the name of Islam need to ensure that after being elected, they remain well-wishers of the deen and Muslims.

I request dua to be made that Allah ﷻ makes me (i.e. the venerable author) a true Muslim and grants me death on Imaan. *Ameen Ya Rabbal-Aalameen.*

Chapter Two

Objections & Answers

All of the objections raised on this issue are due to the objectors having not understood the subject matter completely. They cannot differentiate between Allah's ﷻ dominion and the kingship of the Holy Prophet ﷺ, and so they shout out, "If Rasoolullah ﷺ is the king of the worlds, what remains for Allah ﷻ?!" or "If the Prophet ﷺ is also the king, it would mean that there are two Kings, or that Rasoolullah ﷺ is independent of Allah ﷻ."

Even though I've already explained this difference in the first chapter, I'll answer it at a later stage once more. For now, we'll discuss the objections on this issue put forward until now. If more are raised at a later stage, I will add them here.

Objection 1 The Holy Quran states,

"(O Prophet ﷺ,) Say, 'I neither say to you that I possess the treasures of Allah ﷻ."
– Surah Anaam, Verse 50

We come to know from this verse that the Prophet ﷺ has nothing. How then can we accept him as a king?

Answer – There are a few replies to this objection,

1. In this verse, being the king of the treasures is not negated. Rather, continuously claiming to be so is what is being nullified. In other words, the Prophet ﷺ is saying, "I don't continuously remind you that Allah's ﷻ treasures are with me," because only he who has no control and restraint makes continuous claim. Just as how Allah ﷻ granted the Prophet ﷺ an extreme kingship, so too did He bestow him with colossal control and immense restraint. The strength of a lock put on a treasury is in accordance to the wealth within it, and the tongue is the door to the heart.

2. It's possible that in this verse, the Prophet ﷺ *physically being with the treasures* is what is being negated, not that he's not the king of these things. The goods are in the supervision of a treasurer, but the treasure is definitely under the command of the king. A king doesn't

walk around with his treasures, but declares it to whoever he wants (and thereafter the treasurer distributes it). So, in this verse, the Holy Prophet ﷺ is saying, "I'm the king, not the treasurer." Have you not read that on the mere gesture of the Prophet ﷺ, clouds formed and rainfall occurred?

3. The Kuffaar and Hypocrites are the ones who are being addressed in this verse. They're being told, "O Munaafiqs (Hypocrites), you are all rogues, and treasures are hidden from such people." Secrets of treasures are only disclosed to close confidants. As Muslims, we are told, "I have been granted the keys to the treasures of the earth." The reference for this Hadith has already been presented.

4. 'The treasures of Allah ﷻ' refers to creating/bringing into reality objects which are non-existent. The Holy Quran states,

> "And there is not a thing but its (sources and) treasures (inexhaustible) are with us; but we only send down thereof in due and ascertainable measures."
> – Surah Hijr, Verse 21

This verse doesn't mean that all things are in a specific place from where they come out. No, it means that Allah ﷻ has the power to create every object and continuously create it. So, the Noble Messenger ﷺ is commanded in the first verse to say, "I don't have with me the Divine power to create (i.e. I'm not the Creator)." Refer to *Roohul-Bayaan* under this verse.

Objection 2 The Holy Quran states,

> "(O Prophet ﷺ,) Say, 'I am not independent for doing good and bad to my own self but as Allah ﷻ pleases.'"
> – Surah Aaraaf, Verse 188

This proves that the Holy Prophet ﷺ is not the king over good or bad, even to himself. What will he give others?

Answer – The objector didn't pay attention to the last part, "but as Allah ﷻ pleases." The intent of this verse is, "Without the wish of Allah ﷻ, I am not the commander over any good or bad. Yes, by His desire and bestowal, I am." Self-given kingship is refuted, but bestowed kingship isn't, and this is our belief. It's surprising that an ordinary magistrate can cause harm by sending a person to jail but the Beloved of Allah ﷺ is not the giver of any benefit or harm whatsoever!

Objection 3 Allah ﷻ states,

> "Say, "If I had that thing for which you are hastening, the matter would have been decided between me and you."
> – Surah Anaam, Verse 58

This establishes that the Prophet ﷺ doesn't have the power to bring punishment on anyone, which is why he's demonstrating his helplessness here. The non-Muslims were asking for punishment to befall them and the Prophet ﷺ said this to them in reply. The Quran also states,

> "And if their turning away of faces has grieved you, then if you could, seek a tunnel in the earth or a ladder unto Heaven and bring a sign for them."
> – Surah Anaam, Verse 35

It's proven here too that the Holy Prophet ﷺ cannot cause ruin to anyone and doesn't have the power to bring punishment. The intention of Rasoolullah ﷺ was for all people to become Muslims, but this didn't happen. In fact, he was stopped from having such a desire. Likewise, he desired Imaan for Abu Talib but was told,

> "Undoubtedly, it is not so that you may guide whomsoever you wish on your own accord. Yes, Allah ﷻ guides whoever He wills."
> – Surah Qasas, Verse 56

From this, we come to know that the Prophet ﷺ doesn't have the ability to grant anyone salvation.

Answer – This objection has been made because, again, the opposition has understood the Prophet's ﷺ kingship to be *mustaqil* (independent, permanent) in comparison to Allah's ﷻ while this is not our claim. These verses negate permanent, independent kingship and control, meaning the Prophet ﷺ is being told (regarding the first verse quoted), "Although affairs are steady in my control and I can emplace them, Allah ﷻ doesn't wish for punishment to befall you now, so it won't." Concerning the second verse, he's being told, "It's not the wish of Allah ﷻ that they be shown miracles to their liking." And concerning the third, the Prophet ﷺ is teaching, "Abu Talib demonstrating Imaan cannot be done by me, so if I was not dependant on Allah ﷻ, I would have completed these things myself."

Today, we cannot do anything about things we are the owners of (e.g. land, goods, etc.) without the wish of Allah ﷻ. The Holy Quran states,

> *"You people cannot wish for anything without Allah's ﷻ pleasure."*
> – Surah Dahr, Verse 30

This doesn't necessitate that we are not the owners of our belongings, but that ultimate control is for Allah ﷻ and ours is simply metaphorical with no reality in contrast to the first. Likewise, concerning the third verse quoted, what's being said is, "O Beloved ﷺ, you cannot give salvation to whoever We don't wish it for." This has been explained in this verse,

> *"And Allah ﷻ guides whom He wills to the straight path."*
> – Surah Baqarah, Verse 213

If this wasn't the case, what will this verse mean,

> *"Undoubtedly, this Quran guides to the path that is the most correct."*
> – Surah Bani Israel, Verse 9

The verse cited by the opposition states that none besides Allah ﷻ grants salvation, but in the above verse, we are told that the Quran also grants salvation. Allah ﷻ even states,

> *"And certainly you (O Muhammad ﷺ) guide to the straight path."*
> – Surah Shuraa, Verse 52

No one grants salvation independently. They only do it through the bestowal of Allah ﷻ. After that, both the Quran and the Quran-personified (Muhammad Mustapha ﷺ) have the authority to do so.

It's also been said in Surah Anaam, Verse 35, "O Prophet ﷺ, without Our wish, you cannot do it." We also say that a king cannot benefit or harm anyone without the consent of Allah ﷻ. This is absolutely correct (even though the king *is* able to cause harm or benefit to his servants). Otherwise, what would be the difference between ruler and subjects? This is what's being discussed here. Without comparison, just as how a king is dependant on Allah ﷻ while being the fulfiller of needs for his subjects, so too is the Beloved Prophet ﷺ dependent on Allah ﷻ while being the fulfiller of needs for the creation. Rasoolullah ﷺ is the servant of the Supreme Master but he's also the master of all the servants of the Supreme.

Important Note – Respect must be observed when asking a question. Saying whatever comes to mind is a sign of being deprived of Divine mercy. Rasoolullah ﷺ is the servant of Allah ﷻ and He is his master. Allah ﷻ can speak to His beloveds (such as in the Quran) in whatever way He wishes, and they can demonstrate their humility and dependency on Him in whatever way they wish. What gives us slaves the right to attack these blessed personalities?

Objection 4 The Holy Quran states,

> *"Whether you ask for forgiveness for them or not, it is the same. Even if you ask for forgiveness for them 70 times, Allah ﷻ will never forgive them."*
> – Surah Tauba, Verse 80

This verse proves that if the Holy Prophet ﷺ makes dua for Hypocrites, Allah ﷻ will not accept it. So, where is this closeness and kingship you speak of now?

Answer – Actually, this verse proves the lofty status of the Holy Prophet ﷺ, because it speaks about those who caused sorrow to him by taunting his sincere servants. This is why the verse before it is,

> *"Those who find fault with believers who give charity willingly…"*
> – Surah Tauba, Verse 79

We come to know that these people are criminals in the prophetic court, and so the following has been commanded about them, "O Beloved ﷺ, they have caused sorrow to you, so We will not pardon their faults." We can now conclude that the case of a person who is a criminal in the Holy Prophet's ﷺ court will not be appealed for anywhere else nor gain protection from another source. Even the verse after it states,

> *"This is because they have rejected Allah ﷻ and His Messenger ﷺ."*
> – Surah Tauba, Verse 80

It is the demand of a lover's love to not forgive he who has committed crimes against his beloved. Rasoolullah ﷺ is the Mercy unto the Worlds, and this mercy is unrestricted. No matter how grave the sin, he doesn't hesitate in forgiving it. *It's Allah's ﷻ love* that doesn't forgive such criminals for showing injustice to His Beloved ﷺ. For Him not to forgive such people is displaying honour to the Noble Messenger ﷺ.

Whoever is caught by the contempt of Allah ﷻ can be saved from His wrath by the Holy Prophet's ﷺ intercession, but who will intercede for the one caught by the anger of Rasoolullah ﷺ? It's for this reason that the Sufiya state,

"You can come to the Almighy's ﷻ court with frenzied passion, but when you come to the Holy Prophet ﷺ, be mindful of his court too."

In this court, the simple act of speaking loudly causes your good deeds to be nullified. Some pious elders have said, 'Anal-Haqq' (I am the Truth) in their state of passion, but until today, no-one has ever said, 'Ana Muhammad ﷺ.' (I am Muhammad ﷺ).

Objection 5 The Holy Quran states,

"This matter is not in your hands, whether He forgives them or punishes them, because they are unjust."
– Surah Aale-Imran, Verse 128

The Holy Prophet ﷺ supplicated for the non-Muslims of the Bie're-Ma'oona but was stopped from doing so. If he is the king and his every utterance is accepted in the Divine court, what will this verse mean?

Answer – This verse again demonstrates the glory of the Holy Prophet ﷺ. If someone beloved makes dua for something which is contrary to Divine will, the Divine habit is to stop him from making such a dua. So, it's said, "O Beloved ﷺ, your request is contrary to Our will, and anything being against Our will is impossible. We don't wish for your request to be nullified, so don't make dua on this issue." This verse speaks of the honour possessed by the prophets. Today we supplicate for thousands of things yet nothing happens. The prophets, however, are stopped from making duas which cannot be answered. Hadrat Ibrahim ﷺ wished to make dua for the nation of Lut but was told,

"O Ibrahim ﷺ, do not seek this. Undoubtedly, the

command of your Lord has come. And no doubt, a torment is to approach them that cannot be averted."
– Surah Hūd, Verse 76

Similarly, Rasoolullah ﷺ was stopped from this dua, and stopping him from dua is a great honour for him.

Objection 6 The Holy Quran states,

"I follow only that which is revealed to me."
– Surah Yunus, Verse 15

The Prophet ﷺ couldn't say anything from his own self. Rather, he would give instruction only from revelation. You claim that he is the commander of rulings, so what about this verse? It proves that he's a helpless bondsman like us.

Answer – You haven't read the complete verse,

'Say (O Beloved ﷺ), "It is not for me to change it on my own accord. I only follow what is revealed to me."
– Surah Yunus, Verse 15

The background of this verse is that Aas ibn Waail once said to the Holy Prophet ﷺ, "If you change this Quran or bring another one, we will bring Imaan on you." So, the Prophet ﷺ is being told by Allah ﷻ in this verse, "Say, "I pass on only that which comes to me from my Lord. I cannot lessen anything by myself the way the scholars of the Jews have done." For this reason, 'I only follow' here refers to passing on the Holy Quran without any alteration (i.e. "I relay only that which comes."). 'On my own accord' gestures towards the fact that the Quran itself cannot be changed by the Prophet's ﷺ opinion. Yes, his opinion can be presented before Allah ﷻ for the Quran to change. Quranic verses being revealed according to the desire of the Holy Prophet ﷺ, or 'changed' (i.e. annulled) has occurred several times. A few examples follow,

1. Baitul-Muqaddas (Jerusalem) was the initial qiblah of Muslims, but the desire of the Holy Prophet ﷺ was that the Kaaba be the qibla instead. One day, Rasoolullah ﷺ repeatedly lifted his blessed face towards the Heavens to look (meaning he was awaiting the command for the qiblah to change). This action of his was so beloved to Allah ﷻ that He then revealed,

> *"Surely We have observed you turning your face towards the Heavens repeatedly and We will surely turn you to a qiblah with which you will be pleased."*
> – Surah Baqarah, Verse 144

"We will make the Kaaba the qiblah because it's your desire and happiness." This *naskh* (abrogation) occurred for Rasoolullah's ﷺ pleasure.

Under the commentary of verse 148 of Surah Baqarah, *Tafseer Roohul-Ma'aani* states, "Every nation – in fact, everything – has its own qiblah (direction) towards which it focuses its attention. The qiblah of the angels, dua & souls is Baitul-Ma'moor, the Heaven and the Sidratul-Muntahaa respectively. The qiblah of the Prophet's ﷺ blessed body is the Kaaba, and Allah ﷻ is the qiblah of his soul. The qiblah of the Lord is Muhammad Mustapha ﷺ, the Beloved himself. Allah's ﷻ mercy is constantly focused on him." In short, the changing of the qiblah took place because of Rasoolullah ﷺ.

2. The following verse was initially revealed,

> *"Whether you show what is within your hearts or conceal it, Allah ﷻ will bring you to account for it."*
> – Surah Baqarah, Verse 284

It states that the thought of the heart will also have to be accounted for. However, the wish of the Prophet ﷺ was for Allah ﷻ not to take account of them because they are not within a person's control, and so the following verse was later revealed,

> *"Allah ﷻ places not a burden on any soul but to the extent of his strength."*
> – Surah Baqarah, Verse 286

It can be concluded from this that the bad thoughts which uncontrollably come to the heart are forgiven.

3. During Hajj, the Holy Prophet ﷺ made dua for all the sins of a Haaji to be forgiven. Allah's ﷻ command came that all sins will be forgiven except those related to *Huqooqul-Ibaad* (the rights of the creation). In Muzdalifa, the Prophet ﷺ supplicated for Allah ﷻ to also forgive

the rights of the creation on a Haaji, and so the command came that they too were forgiven.

There are many other examples of these.

Another answer to this objection is that "I only follow…" means whatever the Prophet ﷺ speaks is *wahi* (revelation). This is why it's permissible for the Quran to be annulled by a *Hadith-e-Mutawaatir* (a successive narration of Hadith), and in several instances, the Prophet ﷺ excluded certain people from Quranic commands. References on this subject have already been presented. If the quoted verse in the objection is given the meaning, "I follow only the Quran," then even the Hadith will be refuted by it.

Objection 7 The Holy Prophet ﷺ freed the prisoners of Badr after accepting *fidya* (monetary compensation) from them, causing Divine reproach and Allah ﷻ demonstrating His displeasure towards it. If Rasoolullah ﷺ was the commander of rulings, he would've had the power to do as he pleases. Why would this blessed action cause any reproach? (Surah Anfaal, Verse 68)

Answer – This verse again proves the kingship of the Noble Messenger ﷺ. The explanation of this incident is as follows,

1. If Rasoolullah ﷺ was a helpless servant, he wouldn't have taken fidya and freed the prisoners without first awaiting revelation. We can deduce from this that it was his blessed habit to enforce rulings according to his wish. This was why the above occurred.

2. If the Prophet ﷺ was not the commander of rulings, this decision would have been wrong and the money received in fidya would've been returned to the Kuffaar of Makkah or destroyed, since it is impermissible to use wealth obtained from illegal means. Allah ﷻ would've also prohibited taking fidya in future. But this was not the case. In fact, the money remained Halaal for Muslims,

> "Then eat of what you have obtained as spoils of war."
> – Surah Anfaal, Verse 69

In fact, after the revelation of the quoted verse, the fidya of Hadrat Abbas ؓ and Hadrat Abul-A's ؓ (the husband of the daughter of the Holy Prophet ﷺ, Sayyidah Zainub ؓ) was taken with the following rule emplaced on Muslims, "If Muslims wish, they can free prisoners after taking fidya from them." The Quran states,

> "And afterwards release them either by grace or for ransom."
> – Surah Muhammad, Verse 4

Even though this verse was also annulled according to Hanafi scholars, it was a rule enforced at that time. It is indeed strange that according to the dissenters, reproach was made for taking the fidya while using it was also permitted and later enforced.

3. If Allah ﷻ was displeased with this accepting of fidya, why did He allow it to be taken in the first place? Why didn't He reveal this verse and stop the Muslims from the onset?

Now follows an example to understand the answer to this objection: I can sell the property or house that belongs to me, but sometimes the government stops the sale. At times, it can even return the house sold and classify the sale as impermissible. The government also has the power to take over property when necessary. This doesn't mean that my home or property is not in my control, but that the domain and power of the government is greater than mine.

Without comparison, this decision of the Holy Prophet ﷺ was enforced without Allah's ﷻ decision first. The decision was emplaced but the Prophet ﷺ was reminded that he didn't ratify the decision. In short, this verse is a proof of the Holy Prophet's ﷺ kingship.

Objection 8 When the Kuffaar demanded that the Prophet ﷺ bring out a mountain of gold, an orchard of fruit and springs gushing forth, he replied,

> "Who am I but a being sent by Allah ﷻ?"
> – Surah Bani Israel, Verse 93

In other words, he displayed helplessness. If the Prophet ﷺ was the king of creation, he would've demonstrated these things. What need was there in displaying helplessness?

Answer – The Kuffaar's intention behind these demands was, "O Muhammad! If you do these things, we will bring Imaan on you. If you don't, we won't become Muslims." In other words, they made prophethood dependant and a condition of these things. This verse explains the error of their reasoning. Prophethood is not dependant on these things, that whoever displays them is a prophet and whoever doesn't bring forth mountains of gold isn't. Prophethood is, in fact, an epithet of human qualities (i.e. "I have claimed prophethood, not Divinity."). We accept the kingship of the Prophet ﷺ in both worlds not solely based on his prophethood. Rather, we accept his kingship because of the proofs which are presented in the first chapter.

On this occasion (mentioned in the objection), the Holy Prophet ﷺ said, "Who am I but a being sent by Allah ﷻ?" However, on several other occasions, he unreservedly demonstrated major miracles when people asked for them (e.g. he split the moon in two, gave life to the dead, brought back the set sun, etc.) If he was a helpless servant, why did he demonstrate these miracles? The reason behind this is that those who deemed these actions as the sole yardstick of prophethood were prohibited (from witnessing them), but those who wished to view the Divinely-bestowed kingship were not. A sound Hadith states, "If I wish, mountains of gold can walk with me." We can ascertain that the Prophet ﷺ has power over doing such a thing but simply doesn't wish to demonstrate it.

Objection 9 During the initial stage of his propagation, the Holy Prophet ﷺ said, "O Fathima ؔ, ask of whatever wealth of mine you wish, but I cannot remove the anger of Allah ﷻ from you." When the Prophet ﷺ cannot remove hardship from his beloved daughter, how can he remove our afflictions? How then is his kingship established?

Answer – In this narration, permanent and self-bestowed kingship is what is being negated. In other words, the Prophet ﷺ is saying, "O Fathima ؔ, if you don't accept Imaan, and Allah's ﷻ intention is that you face retribution because of it, then in opposition to Him I cannot remove any hardship from you." The purpose of saying this was to make others understand something, which is why the words 'the anger of Allah ﷻ' was mentioned. It's not the belief of any Muslim that any of us will be able to oppose Allah ﷻ, and whatever is done by a person is carried out by the Divinely-bestowed power and will.

Once again, all of these objections are based on the refuter not comprehending the kingship of the Holy Prophet ﷺ and not differentiating between self-bestowed & independent (Zaati & Mustaqil) and bestowed & dependant (Ataa'i and Ghair-Mustaqil).

Allama Shaami ؔ states that the Hadith means, "Without Allah ﷻ making me the king, I wouldn't have been able to remove any hardship from you."

When the Prophet ﷺ will cause benefit to ordinary people through intercession, why would he deprive his close, believing relatives? A Hadith states, "All bonds and relationships are severed by death except my bond and relationship." This is why Hadrat Umar ؓ made Nikah with Sayyidah Umme-Kulthum bint Fathima bint Rasoolullah ﷺ, so that affinity (by marriage) to the Prophet ﷺ would be attained. The family bond of Rasoolullah ﷺ is excluded from the verse, "When the trumpet is sounded, the family bonds of people will break." – *Raddul-Muhtaar, Vol. 1, Discussion on Ghusl of the Mayyit*

This extract of *Shaami* establishes that Sayyidah Fathima ؓ has immense glory, and that only the family relation to the Holy Prophet ﷺ will be useful on condition that one is a believer.

The Prophet ﷺ states, "The small amount of charity given by my Companions is greater than others giving entire mountains of gold in charity." – *Mishkaat, Baabu Fadhaailis-Sahaabah*

When this is the rank of the Prophet's ﷺ Companions, surely only Allah ﷻ knows the eminence of Sayyidah Fathima Zahra ؓ, the coolness of her father's eyes.

Objection 10 The Ahadith prove that on several occasions, issues were presented to the Holy Prophet ﷺ yet he didn't give his own decision on them but rather waited for revelation (e.g. the changing of the qiblah, when his wife Sayyidah Aisha ؓ was made the target of accusations, etc). If he was the commander of rulings, he would've given his ruling on these things.

Answer – In these events, out of some wisdom, Rasoolullah ﷺ didn't use the direction of his kingship. Rather, he took Allah's ﷻ decision directly. These events had many secrets to them, i.e. the dissenters of the time wouldn't have had a chance to object to his ruling, and/or the importance of the issue is known, etc.

When accusations were leveled against Sayyidah Aisha ؓ, if the Prophet ﷺ did give a decision on the matter himself, the Hypocrites would've said, "He takes his wife's part."

Also, Sayyidah Aisha ؓ would also not have been able to attain the distinction of the Holy Quran proclaiming her greatness and modesty. Now, until Qiyaamat, every reciter of the Holy Quran will recite this verse!

Similarly, if the Noble Messenger ﷺ changed the qiblah on his own accord, the Hypocrites would've said, "Has he changed the qiblah of the prophets?!" So, Allah ﷻ Himself changed the qiblah and took the responsibility of doing so,

> "We will make that with which you are content to be the qiblah."
> - Surah Baqarah, Verse 144

Will anyone now object to Allah's ﷻ doing?

When Rasoolullah ﷺ married Sayyidah Zainab ؓ (the former wife of Hadrat Zaid ؓ), people objected, but Allah ﷻ answered them by saying,

> "We have made the nikah of [Our Beloved ﷺ] to [Zainub ؓ]."
> - Surah Ahzaab, Verse 37

Whoever wishes to object to this should object to Allah ﷻ. Sayyidah Zainub ؓ would say, "Parents make the nikah of their children, but my nikah took place in the Heavens."

From these events, not only is the kingship of the Prophet ﷺ established, but his belovedness is too.

When we sell our minor possessions, there's no need for witnesses and registration of the sale, but in the case of major possessions, such as a house or property, the sale is not done without registering it. We are the owners of both types of possession, but when there is fear of dispute occurring, we make the government responsible for the sale. Allah ﷻ has Himself taken on certain issues while His Beloved ﷺ gave rulings on thousands of others.

The Holy Prophet ﷺ is reported to have said, "Today I have caught Shaitaan, and if I tied him against a pillar, the children of Madina would've been able to play with him, but I remembered the supplication of Sulaiman عليه السلام,

> "(O My Lord), Grant me a kingdom which suits not another after me."
> - Surah Saad, Verse 35

"Therefore, I let him go."

We can deduce that the kingship of Rasoolullah ﷺ is upon jinns, humans, the winds…in fact, the entire creation, but he chose not to demonstrate this because this kingship had become a special and unique miracle of Hadrat Sulaiman ﷺ.

Objection 11 If the Prophet ﷺ was the king of the entire creation, why didn't he lead a life of ease and comfort? Why put himself in constant struggle and hardship?

Answer – The Holy Prophet ﷺ didn't use his kingship for himself. That doesn't mean he didn't have a kingship. During a fast, we don't use the water or food in our homes, not because we are not the owners of these things, but because eating or drinking at this time is contrary to the pleasure of Allah ﷻ.

The Holy Prophet ﷺ didn't use worldly objects for himself. Rather, all the objects and possessions of this world sacrificed themselves for him; and through his blessings, his slaves will also attain these objects and possessions. Rasoolullah's ﷺ life is a model for the entire world, and both rich and poor exist within it. If he spent his lifetime in luxury, who would be the example for the destitute? Therefore, he sometimes accepted money, showed gratitude to Allah ﷻ and distributed it as charity; setting an example for the rich (how to be when attaining wealth and spending it), while at other times, he didn't accept wealth and displayed patience; doing this as a lesson for the poor.

Subhanallah! In one battle, the Prophet ﷺ tied a stone to his blessed stomach. Hadrat Jabir ﷺ invited him for a meal while he was in this state but the Prophet ﷺ then fed *hundreds* of his Companions from only a small amount of food! The reference to this has already been presented. In short, this life of the Holy Prophet ﷺ was not because of helplessness. The fact of the matter is,

> *'He is the king of both worlds, even though he keeps nothing with him. The blessings of both worlds are found in his empty hands.'*
> – Alahazrat Imam Ahmed Raza Khan ﷺ

A *bakheel* (miser) is someone who neither eats nor gives others to eat. A *sakhi* (generous person) is one who eats himself and feeds others, but a *jawaad* (magnanimous) person is someone who doesn't eat himself but still feeds others. This is why Allah ﷻ is not called 'sakhi', but 'Jawaad'. He doesn't eat Himself but gives others to eat, and Rasoolullah ﷺ is the manifestation of this quality. – *Tafseer Roohul-Bayaan*

Whatever and whenever he does eat is only for the education of his Ummah. Otherwise, he has absolutely no need for it. In fact, food and eating is needy of him. Rasoolullah ﷺ is not needy of anything besides Allah ﷻ. He once said, "Who from amongst you is like me? My Lord feeds me unseen sustenance and gives me to drink."

When the hardship of hunger appears, it's due to a person's humanity emanating from within, while fasting continuously is the emanation of one's *nooraniyyat* (being of noor). In Khaibar, the poison didn't cause any effect to the Prophet ﷺ, but its impact was felt at the time of his demise (i.e. at the time of his humanity becoming visible). This is a very intricate issue. Refer to *Mirqaat Sharah Mishkaat, Tafseer Roohul-Bayaan* or *Lam'aat* for a detailed explanation to it.

و صلى الله تعالى على سيدنا محمد و اله و صحبه اجمعين
امين برحمتك يا ارحم الراحمين

Closing statements Those who benefit from this treatise are requested to remember this beggar (Mufti Ahmed Yaar Khan ؓ) in their duas for death with Imaan. Please supplicate that Allah ﷻ accepts these books of mine and makes them a means of perpetual blessings and provisions for the Hereafter for me. Also, make dua that the shadow of mercy of my Murshid and master, Sadrul-Afaadil Maulana Sayed Muhammad Naeemuddin Qibla ؓ remains on me and the entire Ahle-Sunnah.

Ahmed Yaar Khan Naeemi Ashrafi

Note This book was written during the lifetime of Hadrat Sadrul-Afaadil ؓ, and so the above dua was made for him. Hadrat's demise has now occurred. We now make dua that Allah ﷻ envelops his blessed grave with Noor and grants us barkat through his blessings. *Ameen.*

www.ingramcontent.com/pod-product-compliance
Lightning Source LLC
Chambersburg PA
CBHW031430040426
42444CB00006B/761